HOPPING AHEAD OF CLIMATE CHANGE

Snowshoe Hares, Science, and Survival

SNEED B. COLLARD III

www.buckinghorsebooks.com

Distributed by Mountain Press Publishing Company, Missoula, MT 800-234-5308
www.mountain-press.com

Collard, Sneed B., author.
　　　Hopping ahead of climate change : snowshoe hares,
　　science, and survival / by Sneed B. Collard III.
　　pages cm
　　Includes index.
　　SUMMARY: Scientists seek to answer the critical question:
　　Can snowshoe hares and other animals with seasonal coat color
　　changes adapt to shorter winters caused by climate change?
　　Audience: Ages 10-16.
　　LCCN 2016907272
　　ISBN 978-0-9844460-8-7

　　1. Snowshoe rabbit--Climatic factors--Juvenile literature.
　　2. Climatic changes--Juvenile literature.
　　3. Acclimatization--Juvenile literature. [1. Showshoe rabbit.
　　　2. Climatic changes. 3. Hares.
　　4. Acclimatization.]   I. Title.

　　QL737.L32C655 2016　　　　599.32'8
　　　　　　　　　QBI16-600077

Cover and book design by Kathleen Herlihy-Paoli, Inkstone.
The text of this book is set in Simoncini Garamond.

Photo Credits
• L. Scott Mills Research Photos: Front Cover (right, left top and
  bottom), Front Flap, Back Cover, 3 (top, third, fourth), 4-5, 25-31, 36, 38, 41
  (snowshoe & mountain hares), 45, 46 (all hares), 49 (top), 61
• US Fish and Wildlife Service: 9 (Canada lynx), 41 (white-tailed jackrabbit by
  Biggins Dean), 41 & 46 (long-tailed weasel by Melanie Olds, used under the
  Creative Commons Attribution-Share Alike 2.0 Generic license)
• US Geological Survey: 17 (polar bears by Mike Lockhart)
• Steve Running: 32
• Dick Moberg: 41, 45, 46 (Arctic foxes)
• Andy Howard: 46, 49 (rock ptarmigans)
• Alpsdake: 41 (Japanese hare, used under Creative Commons Attribution-Share
  Alike 3.0 Unported license)
• Eleassar: 41 (Djungarian hamster, used under the Creative Commons
  Attribution-Share Alike 2.5 Generic license)
• All other photos by Sneed B. Collard III

Manufactured in the United States of America

10 9 8 7 6 5 4 3 2 1

Bucking Horse Books
MISSOULA, MONTANA

For Owen,
Who keeps us hopping ahead
of the curve.
Love,
Uncle Sneed

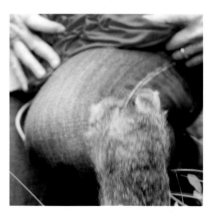

❯ *Opposite (top to bottom):*
Snowshoe hare
Coal-fired power plant
Snowshoe hare
Scientist Marketa Zimova
Leveret (young snowshoe hare)

CONTENTS

Light Bulbs with Legs

It's late October. Almost Halloween. Dawn breaks across the northern Rocky Mountains and a snowshoe hare hops through the forest in search of food. It pauses frequently to nibble on grasses, leaves, and the twigs of low-growing fir and larch trees. Although the sky is light, the hare does not seem overly concerned about getting eaten. This time of year, its dazzling white coat blends in perfectly with snow. This camouflage provides excellent protection against lynx, coyotes, marten, and other predators. Unfortunately, this year, the hare has a problem.

There is no snow.

As it shuffles along, its white coat sticks out like a glowing light bulb against the rich browns and greens of the forest floor.

A great horned owl notices.

As the hare hops across a small clearing, the owl leaps from its perch. On silent wings, it sweeps through the air in a deadly arc. At the last moment, the hare spots the owl and springs to escape.

Too late.

The predator pounces on its prey, making a quick kill. For the owl, it is an easy meal. For the hare, it's a disaster—one that casts doubt on the species' future survival.

Chapter One

The Cheeseburger of the Forest

Scott Mills parks his truck near one of his favorite study areas, just outside of Seeley Lake, Montana. "This place is a hotbed for hares," he points out. "Not only is there a good number of hares here but for hare country, it's pretty forgiving. It's flat, which makes it a lot easier to hike around in winter and summer. It also makes tracking the hares easier."

The previous night, Scott set up more than two dozen live animal traps in the surrounding fir and spruce forest. Now, he is about to see if his efforts have paid off.

Following pink plastic flagging that he has tied to tree branches, he bushwhacks from one trap to the next. The first three sit empty. As he approaches the fourth trap, Scott grins and exclaims, "Got one!"

What the hare doesn't know is that she is about to become part of a worldwide scientific study—one that could help save not only snowshoe hares, but dozens of other animal species.

❮ *Biology professor Scott Mills prepares for a morning of trapping, weighing, collaring, and tagging snowshoe hares in his study site near Seeley Lake, Montana.*

A Hare-y Interest

A wildlife biologist at the University of Montana, Scott Mills first took an interest in snowshoe hares in 1998. Back then, one of the hare's major predators, the Canada lynx, was listed as a threatened species by the US government. Since lynx depend on snowshoe hares more than any other food source, scientists also became concerned about hare populations.

Scott applied for and received grant money to study snowshoe hares in Montana and other parts of the lynx's US range. He especially wanted to discover whether logging and other human activities might affect hare numbers—and, in turn, harm lynx populations.

"What that means," Scott half-jokes, "is that I spent the next ten years learning how many different ways hares can die."

The Perfect Prey

"Hares don't die of old age," Scott explains. "Anything that eats meat in the forest feeds on snowshoe hares. Coyote, foxes, bobcats, lynx, owls, goshawks, weasels, marten, fishers—everything. Even some things you don't expect, like red squirrels, feed on newborn hares. I call hares the candy bar of the forest, but my students call them the *cheeseburger* of the forest. A few hares live for four years. A few more live three, and some, two years. Most live only a year or less."

With so many predators trying to make a meal of them, it's not surprising that snowshoe hares have evolved ways to protect themselves. They feed mostly at dawn and dusk, when predators have a harder time seeing them. They remain still as much as possible so that they don't attract attention. More than anything, hares blend in with their surroundings. Most of the year, their brown coats match the brown forest floor. In autumn, shorter days trigger their coats to change, or molt, from brown to white. This

THE LYNX-HARE RELATIONSHIP

In the northern part of their range, lynx and hares have a famous relationship. When hare numbers go up, lynx numbers go up—way up. When hare numbers go down, lynx numbers go down—way down. The cycle is extreme and depends almost entirely on how many hares are born and how many get eaten.

Farther south, the relationship gets more complicated. Lynx still depend on hares just as much as their northern relatives, but the habitat in the south has a bigger mix of dense and thin forests. There are also more species of predators. This provides a greater variety of places where hares can hide, but also more ways and places to get killed. The overall result? The lynx-hare cycles don't reach the extreme highs and lows that they do farther north.

^ *Canada lynx*

‹ *A trapped female snow-shoe hare quietly waits for Scott to process her before releasing her back into the wild.*

camouflages hares against the white, snowy background of the oncoming winter. In the spring, when the snows melt, the hares molt back to brown.

After studying hares for four or five years, however, Scott noticed something disturbing. "I'd be out there in the spring, following hares around, and I'd find a brilliant white hare sitting on brown, bare earth. It was obvious the hare thought it was protected by its camouflage. Instead, it stood out like a sore thumb."

Scott had an idea what might be happening: in some years, winter snows were melting earlier than usual, but the hares were not receiving the message. Why? Because coat color changes are triggered primarily by the *length of the day*, not by actual snow conditions. As a result, the hares stood out like flashing neon billboards. They told every predator in the forest, "EAT ME!"

This led Scott to wonder, "As climate change gets worse and winters grow shorter, will predators take a bigger and bigger toll on snowshoe hares? Will the species even be able to survive?"

⌃ *Dense forest and brush cover provides ideal snowshoe hare habitat.*

Chapter Two

HARES IN A WARMING WORLD

Climate change, often referred to as global warming, is the term scientists use to describe the fact that our planet is growing warmer. Climate change is a complicated topic, but the reasons for it are simple.

Starting in the early 1700s—the dawn of the modern industrial age—humans began burning increasing quantities of fuel. We especially began burning fossil fuels—coal, oil, and natural gas. We used these fuels to heat buildings, generate electricity, and power automobiles and other vehicles. By the late twentieth century and into the twenty-first century, our use of fossil fuels reached astonishing proportions. In the year 2012, for example, the world's coal consumption exceeded *eight billion tons* per year.

Why was that a problem?

When burned, fossil fuels release carbon dioxide (CO_2) and other gases into Earth's atmosphere. These "greenhouse gases" trap heat, driving up our planet's temperatures. Higher temperatures have, in turn, led to changing climate conditions.

❮ *One of thousands of coal-fired power plants that pump carbon dioxide into the atmosphere around the globe.*

The "Other" Greenhouse Gases

Although carbon dioxide plays the most important role in climate change, several other gases make major impacts. These include methane, nitrous oxide, and water vapor. Methane is accidentally released by oil- and gas-drilling activities, and by the digestion of food by livestock. Nitrous oxide is released by manure left on the ground and by the use of artificial fertilizers. A third gas, water vapor, also plays a huge role in trapping heat in the atmosphere. Unfortunately, we can do little about this gas because it naturally increases with air temperatures and is beyond our direct control.

❯ *About 1.4 billion cows populate the planet. According to the UN Food and Agriculture Organization, livestock production releases 35% of the methane and 65% of the nitrous oxide generated by human activities.*

Many scientists consider climate change to be the biggest threat that our planet faces. Warmer temperatures are already leading to:

- rising sea levels
- extreme hurricanes, droughts, floods, and other weather events
- increased wildfire frequency and severity
- greater spread of invasive, or harmful, species
- more human health issues
- increased risk of extinction for many species

Not surprisingly, the effects of climate change vary from place to place. Climate scientists, however, observe one trend almost everywhere on the planet: less snow cover.

^ *Even in the Rocky Mountains, snows are arriving significantly later and melting earlier than they were fifty years ago.*

Waning Winters

"The single biggest signal of climate change globally," Scott explains, "the most consistent one, is not changes in temperature. It's not changes in moisture. Those are sort of high in some places and low in some places. But almost everywhere there's a decrease in duration of snowpack. Whether you are in the Alps, whether you

15 WARMEST YEARS ON RECORD

RANK	YEAR	DEGREES CELSIUS	DEGREES FAHRENHEIT
1	2015	0.90	1.62
2	2014	0.74	1.33
3	2010	0.70	1.26
4	2013	0.66	1.19
5	2005	0.65	1.17
6 (tie)	1998	0.63	1.13
6 (tie)	2009	0.63	1.13
8	2012	0.62	1.12
9 (tie)	2003	0.61	1.10
9 (tie)	2006	0.61	1.10
9 (tie)	2007	0.61	1.10
12	2002	0.60	1.08
13 (tie)	2004	0.57	1.03
13 (tie)	2011	0.57	1.03
15 (tie)	2001	0.54	0.97
15 (tie)	2008	0.54	0.97

This table ranks the 15 warmest years on record since global temperatures were first recorded in 1880. For each year, the last two columns show how much warmer the year was than the average temperature recorded during the twentieth century.

GLOBAL TEMPERATURES JANUARY-DECEMBER, 2015

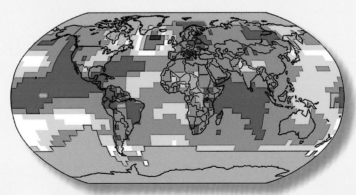

Record Coldest

Much Cooler than Average

Cooler than Average

Near Average

Warmer than Average

Much Warmer than Average

Record Warmest

Source: NOAA's National Centers for Environmental Information, www.ncdc.noaa.gov/sotc/global/201513

▲ *Shrinking polar ice caps pose a grave danger to polar bears, which depend on the sea ice to hunt their seal prey. Polar bears, however, are only one of hundreds—perhaps thousands—of species threatened by climate change.*

are in the Adirondacks, whether you are in the Rockies, Cascades, or any other temperate region of the world, there's a decrease in snow."

One of Scott's colleagues, climate scientist Steve Running, puts it more precisely. "The winter season, with snow on the ground, is on average two to three weeks shorter than the snow cover period fifty years ago. While certain regions can still have an exceptionally cold and snowy winter on occasion, the worldwide averages clearly show winter decreasing."

Only a few regions in the world, such as eastern Antarctica and some very high mountain areas in the Himalayas, are seeing more snow than in the past. Almost everywhere else is receiving less snow, and that is alarming news for snowshoe hares and other animals whose coats change color. It is news that pushed Scott Mills's research into important new directions.

Hare-Raising Questions

Scott's observation of hare "light bulbs" in the forest led him to ask several scientific questions:

1. Were hares really mismatched? In other words, did hares with white coats find themselves sitting on brown backgrounds for any significant lengths of time—and did brown hares find themselves sitting on white backgrounds?

2. Were mismatched hares more likely to get eaten than hares that were camouflaged?

3. Were hares even aware of their mismatch, and if so, did they do anything about it?

4. As Earth's temperatures grow warmer, would hare mismatches increase?

All of these questions were interesting by themselves. Together, they would help Scott and other scientists answer the most important question of

⌃ *Mile-long coal trains such as this one not only supply coal to United States power plants, but to hundreds of power plants in China—the world's largest producer of greenhouse gases.*

‹ *Gasoline-powered automobiles produce almost one-third of global CO_2 emissions, but also require polluting oil refineries such as this one to produce fuel.*

all: Could mismatches due to climate change drive hares and other species to extinction?

Scott was the perfect person to try to answer these questions. During his years working on the lynx-hare relationship, he had learned everything there was to know about studying hares. He and his team could measure births. They could record deaths. They could track hare movements. Now, they could use all of that experience to begin answering questions about hares and climate change.

All they had to do was get hopping.

Chapter Three

STUDYING HARES

Scott and his team have developed a fairly simple approach to studying hares. "We put radio collars on them," Scott explains. "Not fancy satellite collars, just plain radio collars that have a range of one to two kilometers (.6 to 1.2 miles). Then, every single week, our technicians use an antenna to find every single hare. They take a picture of the hare to record its coat color. At the same time, they record the amount of snow around the hare so that we can figure out if there is a mismatch."

Scott's team also records one other thing about each hare: is it even *alive*? "The radio lets us know whether a hare is alive or dead," Scott says. "The collars themselves usually last longer than the hares. The collars last up to about two years, but the hares don't usually survive that long. It's a lucky hare that lasts three years. If it's dead, we go find it and collect the remains so that we can figure out who killed it."

❮ *Radio collars allow scientists to observe snowshoe hares—and tell them when a hare has been eaten by a predator.*

❮ *Even for an experienced scientist, getting a hare out of a trap can be a challenge. This stubborn hare won't budge, so Scott blows on its face to annoy it. Finally, it spins around and runs into a cloth sack.*

❯ *Once a hare is bagged, Scott and other scientists can more easily weigh, measure, and collar it.*

Because so many hares get eaten, Scott's team has to constantly trap and collar new hares. A good hare technician can keep track of fifteen to twenty-five hares at one time. When three or four hares die, the technician traps more and places radio collars on them. Over time, this has allowed Scott's team to collect a huge amount of data about the hares and what is happening to them.

HARES ARE NOT RABBITS!

*W*hen discussing the perils faced by snowshoe hares, Scott often hears statements such as, "Of course these rabbits will be fine because they breed like, well, rabbits!" What many people don't realize is that hares are not rabbits. "One difference," Scott explains, "is that rabbits are born in safer underground burrows while hares are born above ground where they are exposed to predators from birth. Hares also have smaller litter sizes than rabbits, which means they can't reproduce as quickly." Rabbits live in a much wider variety of habitats than hares, and have even adapted to many human habitats such as farms, parks, and vacant lots. All of these differences make hares much more vulnerable than their more popular—and populous—rabbit relatives.

⌃ *Cottontail rabbit*

Three Hare-y Years

From 2010 to 2012, Scott and his team monitored 148 snowshoe hares at their study site in western Montana. They recorded when each hare began molting from brown to white in the fall and from white to brown in the spring. Every week, they also recorded each hare's fur color in 20% increments. In the fall, for instance, a "20% hare" was one with about one-fifth of its body covered in white fur and the rest in brown. On the other hand, an "80% hare" had almost completely finished molting. Its fur was mostly white with only a few patches of brown.

Along with measuring hare coat color, Scott's team measured the percentage of snow cover in a circle with a ten-meter (thirty-three-foot) radius around each hare. This snow cover was also measured in 20% increments.

Scott and his team considered a hare mismatched when the color between its coat and its background differed by at least 60%. For example, if a hare was 60% white and the ground around it was 0% white (bare of snow, or 100% brown), Scott considered that a mismatch. On the other hand, if a hare was 80% white and the ground around it was 40% covered with snow, Scott did not consider that a mismatch.

The years 2010 to 2012 turned out to be very good ones for Scott and his team to do their study. Why? Because this time period included heavy, normal, and light snowfall years. That gave the scientists a good representation of what is really happening in nature.

It also gave them some startling results.

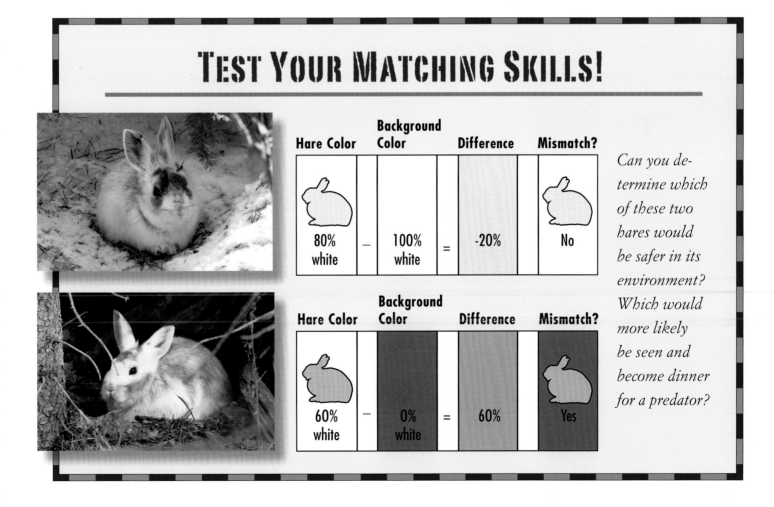

TEST YOUR MATCHING SKILLS!

Hare Color		Background Color		Difference		Mismatch?
80% white	−	100% white	=	-20%		No

Hare Color		Background Color		Difference		Mismatch?
60% white	−	0% white	=	60%		Yes

Can you determine which of these two hares would be safer in its environment? Which would more likely be seen and become dinner for a predator?

Chapter Four

White Hares, Brown Backgrounds

During their three-year study, Scott and his team found that, on average, a hare spent about a week mismatched. It was up to one of Scott's graduate students, Marketa Zimova, to figure out if this mismatch actually posed a problem for the hares. Marketa, who is originally from the Czech Republic, had trapped, collared, and tracked hares in Montana. Now, she had to try to answer the question, do mismatched hares get eaten more often than camouflaged hares?

❯ *Scott's graduate student, Marketa Zimova, extensively worked with the hares in the field before analyzing the lab's three years of field data.*

❮ *This pelt is all that remains of a hare that probably fell victim to an owl.*

WHICH MISMATCH IS DEADLIER?

*H*ares can be mismatched in two ways. They can be white sitting on a brown background or they can be brown sitting on a white background. Is one mismatch more dangerous than the other?

"We study brown on white and white on brown," Scott says. "We call white on brown 'positive mismatch' and brown on white 'negative mismatch,' but we don't yet have enough data to separate those things statistically. Just spending time out in the woods, though, we feel like white on brown is much more notice- able. If you think about it, if you're out there skiing or something, there's pine cones, melted spots, logs, and lots of other brown stuff on snow. So a brown hare sitting on the snow is easy to miss. But when you're out in the spring and there is no snow, and you see a white ball out there, you don't miss it."

Marketa analyzed all of the team's data on hares. She compared survival rates of mismatched hares to those of camouflaged hares. What she learned is that snowshoe hares died during all times of the study years.

However, more hares died during the periods when they were mismatched.

"The more they were mismatched," Marketa explains, "the more likely they were to die. When you're 100% mismatched, your chance of surviving one week is 7% lower than if you are completely camouflaged.

"Spring was the worst," she continues. "It might be because all of these predators are really hungry then, but I'd see a mismatched hare and think, *He's probably going to be dead by next week.* I was usually right."

Clueless Hares

A huge problem, Scott and his team found, is that the hares did not seem to know when they were mismatched. If a white hare sat on a brown patch of ground, but patches of snow existed nearby, the hare seemed to make no effort to go sit on that snow. When Scott or one of his team walked up to a mismatched hare, the animal remained sitting on its brown patch of ground until the person almost stepped on it.

This led Scott to ask himself, "Would the hares behave differently in the presence of a real, wild predator?" To get an idea, Brandon Davis, another of Scott's graduate students, ran an experiment. "What I did," Brandon explains, "is I approached hares with Scott's dog, Sage, on a leash. One person would go in and locate the hare. Then, I would go in with Sage. We let Sage go in first so the hare would react to the dog to see what the hare would do."

How did the hares respond?

They didn't, it turned out. The hares seemed to trust in their camouflage, even if they *weren't* camouflaged.

Still, this might not be a huge problem if the hares could adjust the timing of their molts. If snows came later and the hares could molt later, then the cost of mismatch might not be so high. But could they? Did the hares have any control over the timing of their molt?

Ready, Set, Molt!

When Scott and his team took a close look at their three years of data, they found that in the fall it took a hare about forty days to complete its molt from brown to white. Unfortunately, these dates had almost nothing to do with how much snow had fallen on the ground. Instead, the start and finish dates of the molts depended almost solely on the length of daylight hours.

The situation in spring turned out to be a little better. Alex Kumar, another one of Scott's graduate students, studied hare molting in the Blackfoot River Valley, about thirty miles from Scott's main study site. During

⌃ *Hares are so confident about their camouflage that they often allow predators—including humans—to closely approach.*

SURVIVAL COST OF BEING MISMATCHED

Even under the best circumstances, hare survival is uncertain. With increasing mismatch, a hare's chance of surviving drops dramatically.

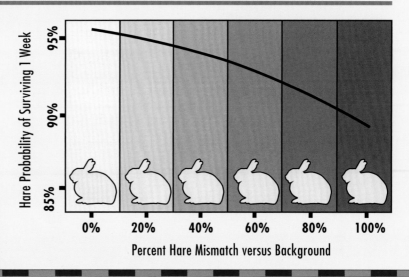

2013 and 2014, Alex discovered that hares had some ability to shift both the timing and speed of their spring molts. "When snow melts early the hares can start their molts a little earlier, and when the snow hangs around they can slam on the brakes and take longer to turn brown," Alex explains. In the early snowmelt year of 2013, for instance, hares completed their molt from white to brown about ten days earlier than in 2014.

Unfortunately, the hares' ability to make small adjustments in spring still isn't always enough to keep them from ending up mismatched. The good news is that, at least for now, the hares in Scott's study areas seem to be holding their own. Even though hares are often mismatched, hare numbers are staying steady or even increasing. But what about the future? If climate change continues to get worse, as most scientists predict, what will that mean for the hares?

Chapter Five

Hare Today, Gone Tomorrow?

A key part of Scott's research has involved predicting how snow cover might change in the future. If the length of time that snow covers the ground doesn't change, then current levels of mismatch might not turn out to be a big problem for snowshoe hare populations. On the other hand, if snow cover keeps decreasing—and mismatches increase—that could trigger a hare population meltdown.

To help him answer the snow cover question, Scott has worked closely with Steve Running and other climate scientists to predict future snow cover in his study area. "We're not just taking some giant computer-generated map of the northwest United States and using that to make predictions," Scott explains. "Instead, we're saying, 'Okay, at the scale of our study area where these animals live, what snow conditions have they faced in the past, and what will they face in the future?' To do that, we use super-complex local weather models

❮ *Scott worked closely with climate scientist Steve Running to create precise models of past and future snow levels in Scott's study areas.*

to estimate future snow cover. Our snow models are telling us what's happening *at that spot* on Earth where those hares are living."

Coming up with these models costs big bucks because it requires a lot of data and computer time. The efforts of Scott's team, however, have allowed him to make solid predictions about what snowshoe hares will experience in the future—and how much they are likely to be mismatched.

The news isn't good.

Hare-y Forecasts

To forecast future snow cover, Scott and his team looked at predictions of carbon dioxide and other greenhouse gases in the atmosphere for the middle and the late twenty-first century. Climate scientists have already estimated these levels based on various factors, including:

- current global consumption of fossil fuels
- predictions of fossil fuels consumption in the future
- how rapidly carbon dioxide is—and will be—removed from the atmosphere by oceans, forests, and other "carbon sinks."

When Scott and his colleagues plugged future carbon dioxide levels into snow models, they found a dramatic increase in the number of days snowshoe hares will be mismatched.

According to these forecasts, if carbon dioxide emissions remain on the lower end of what scientists predict, then the time Scott's snowshoe hares will be mismatched by the middle of the century will increase to about twenty-eight days. By the end of the century, the number of mismatched days will increase to thirty-nine days.

However, if carbon dioxide emissions continue to increase at their current, high rate, the situation will be much worse. In that case, models show that the mismatch will last thirty-five days by mid-century and *sixty-eight days* by the end of the century—almost ten weeks!

HARE MISMATCH BASED ON PREDICTIONS OF FUTURE GREENHOUSE GAS EMISSIONS

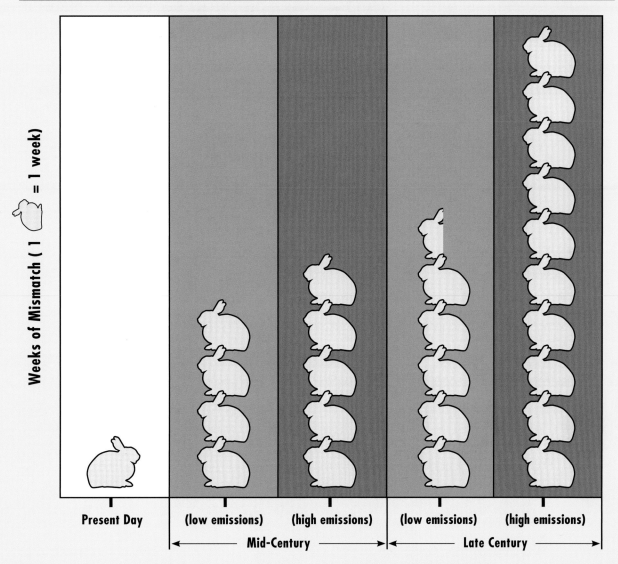

The impact of climate change on snowshoe hares will depend on the amount of snow cover in the future. That, in turn, will depend on how much carbon dioxide and other greenhouse gases humans release into our atmosphere. The green columns above show predictions by Scott's lab on how many weeks hares will be mismatched if humans release smaller amounts of greenhouse gases into the atmosphere. The orange columns show weeks of mismatch if humans release larger amounts of gases. The estimates of future greenhouse gas emissions were established by scientists working closely with a United Nations group called the Intergovernmental Panel on Climate Change, which studies climate change and its effects.

⌃ *Scott's team discovered that even small increases in mismatch duration greatly increase a hare's probability of being killed by a predator.*

What would that mean for the hares?

In both cases, the survival rates of hares would drop significantly. Currently, normal hare survival is about 9.3% per year. In other words, a hare's chances of surviving one year is only 9.3%—less than one in ten. By the end of the century, if greenhouse emissions are on the lower end of what scientists predict, hare survival would drop to 8.0% per year. In the high-emissions case, hare survival would decrease even more—to 7.0% per year.

These changes may seem small, but they point to a deadly conclusion. "If we put the *cost* of being mismatched up against the *increase* in mismatch going into the future," Scott explains, "the lower survival will cause even a healthy hare population—one that is increasing now—to be declining rapidly by the late twenty-first century."

Even Scott was surprised by the results. "It's the kind of thing where you end up rechecking the data again and again," he says, "because it seems amazing. But I'm quite confident in it."

And that leaves only one question: Is there any chance that snowshoe hares and other coat-color-changing animals will survive future changes in climate?

Chapter Six

HOPE FOR HARES

The research conducted by Scott and his team raises concerns not only for snowshoe hares. It spells trouble for many other animal species around the globe. More than twenty species of animals, from lemmings, weasels, and hamsters to Arctic foxes, ptarmigans, and other hare species change their coat colors each fall and spring. The molts of every one of these species is triggered mainly by seasonal day lengths, not by actual snow cover. In other words, every one of these species is likely to find itself mismatched more and more as climate change continues. That will impact both the species themselves and the dozens—perhaps hundreds—of other animals that prey on and interact with these species.

Surprisingly, Scott Mills is optimistic that hares and other species with seasonal coat color changes will find ways to survive. "We actually think that this is a climate change story that does have a lot of hope," Scott says.

❮ *Snowshoe hares are only one species at risk from shorter winters. This mountain hare is one of more than twenty species around the globe that changes its coat color based on the time of the year—not actual snow conditions.*

RANGES OF SEVEN SPECIES WITH SEASONAL COAT COLOR CHANGES

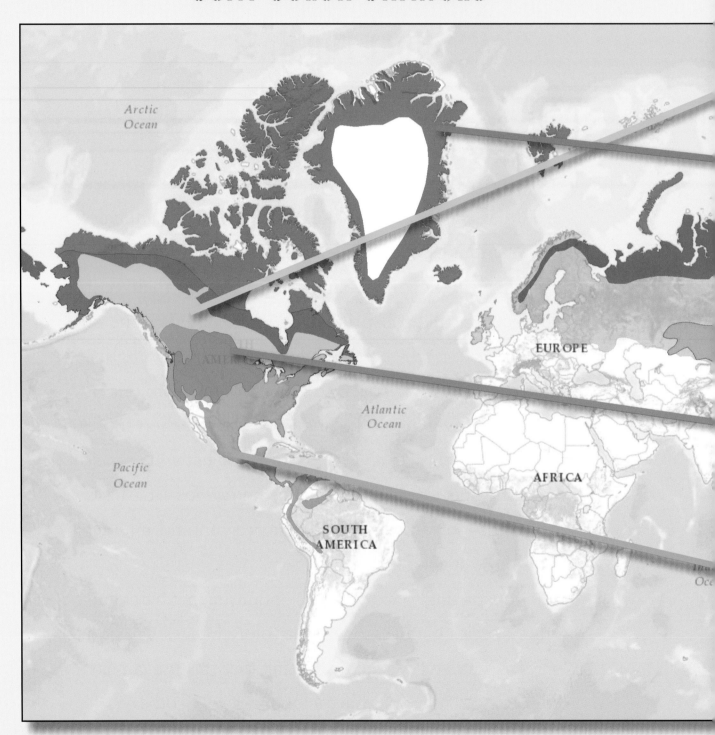

Map created by Eugenia Bragina. Sources: Esri, HERE, DeLorme, Intermap, increment P Corp., GEBCO, USGS, FAO, NPS, NRCAN, GeoBase, IGN, Kadaster NL, Ordinance Survey, Esri Japan, METI, Esri China (Hong Kong), swisstopo, MapmyIndia, © Open StreetMap contributors, and the GIS User Community

Snowshoe Hare

Japanese Hare

Artic Fox

Djungarian Hamster

Mountain Hare

White-tailed Jackrabbit

Long-tailed Weasel

Note: the dark pink color shows the over-lapping range of Arctic foxes and snowshoe hares.

Why?

One reason is natural selection. Natural selection is the ability of certain individuals to survive better than others. In every species, individuals are different. In the case of snowshoe hares, some hares naturally molt earlier and some molt later. As snow cover decreases over time, hares that molt later in the fall and earlier in the spring will most likely survive better than other hares. They will pass their molting traits on to their offspring. The result? Over time, the snowshoe hare species will evolve, or adapt, so that the timing of its molts better matches the changes in snow conditions.

∧ *This hare, dubbed "Sir Robin" by Scott's team, belongs to a population of hares from Washington State that actually stays brown all year long.*

EVOLVE OR ADAPT: WHAT'S THE DIFFERENCE?

The words "evolve" and "adapt" often are used interchangeably—for good reason since the two are closely related. What's the difference? The word "evolve" simply means "to change." For living things, evolution is the process by which we acquire new characteristics that become a part of us, coded into our genes. "Adapt" usually refers to an organism's ability to cope with a specific challenge or change in the environment.

Sometimes, animals can use their intelligence to adapt to a new challenge. If one food source runs out, for instance, some animals may be able to switch to a new food source. Often, however, adaptation happens through the process of natural selection and evolution. Natural selection weeds out organisms that can't cope with a new challenge, leaving a group of survivors that has a better mix of "successful" genes. When these survivors reproduce, the new generation will have actually changed into something slightly different from what came before. Evolution has taken place—and so has adaptation.

An important point to remember about evolution is that a single individual cannot evolve. An individual can survive by having better genes, but its genes cannot improve or change while it's alive. Only when individuals reproduce and pass on their better mix of genes does it change the species—and only then, does evolution take place.

But will this actually happen? Can snowshoe hares and other species evolve fast enough to keep up with climate change?

Hares for All Seasons

The hares' ability to evolve and adapt will depend on their genes, which reside in their DNA. Genes are like little road maps or sets of instructions inside our bodies' cells. They control how we develop, how we grow, how smart we are, the color of our skin, and countless other aspects of our lives.

Here's the problem: if none of the hares in a population contain the genes to molt later or earlier, then that population won't be able to evolve, or adapt. Climate change will snuff it out.

What Scott and other scientists are finding, however, is that different hare populations contain huge warehouses of genetic material. This improves the chances that the molt timing of at least some populations could change with changing snow conditions.

"We have these hares in the Olympic Peninsula in Washington that stay brown all winter long," Scott explains. "We have hares in the Cascade Mountains where there are winter-white and winter-brown hares living together. If you look at every single species—weasels and foxes and hares—throughout their ranges, there are populations that molt brown to white, there are populations that stay brown, and there are at least a few places like the Cascades where there are polymorphic populations—those that have both brown and white animals in the winter. So that right there

WHY DON'T THE HARES JUST MOVE?

*T*alking about mismatched hares raises an obvious question: If snowshoe hares are mismatched in one place, why don't they just move to a snowier place? Unfortunately for hares, that might be easier said than done. "Something about hares," Scott says, "is that they don't tend to move a lot. They're also a mountain species, so they've got this whole valley between them and the next mountain range. In Montana, these valleys are filled with ponderosa pines. Hares don't go there. So there's sort of these island-like conditions that hares live in. I'm not saying there won't be range shifts. Obviously, there's been lots of range shifts of birds and plants. But I think for animals such as the snowshoe hare, movement won't be as much of an option."

❯ Like snowshoe hares, different populations of Arctic foxes have different molt timing. Some even stay brown all winter. This photo was taken by scientists using "camera traps" to study Arctic foxes in Sweden.

tells you that in the past, natural selection has adapted these animals to their local conditions."

Still, this doesn't mean that all populations of animals with seasonal coat color changes will be able to adapt to the extreme climate change that is forecast for the rest of the century. To find out more, Scott's team is expanding its work beyond snowshoe hares, to various animal species around the world.

Chapter Seven

Going Global

Scott and his colleagues have launched several projects to study other species and populations that change their coat colors with the seasons. Scott's graduate student Brandon Davis has begun studying snowshoe hares and weasels in West Virginia and Pennsylvania, where both winter-brown and winter-white populations of these animals live. Because they are so secretive, the weasels pose a special challenge to work on, but Brandon has set up cameras to capture photos of these shy creatures as they go about their business.

In Scotland, Marketa Zimova is working with scientists on the mountain hare. "These hares are different from snowshoe hares," Marketa explains. "They live in open heather moorlands, so you can find them by just walking around." What is unique about this study is that sixty years ago Scottish scientists went out every few days and wrote down the coat colors of the

‹ *Studies on a variety of species will help Scott and other scientists learn more about animals' abilities to adapt to future climate changes. Clockwise from upper left: mountain hare, snowshoe hare, long-tailed weasel, Arctic foxes, rock ptarmigans (summer and winter).*

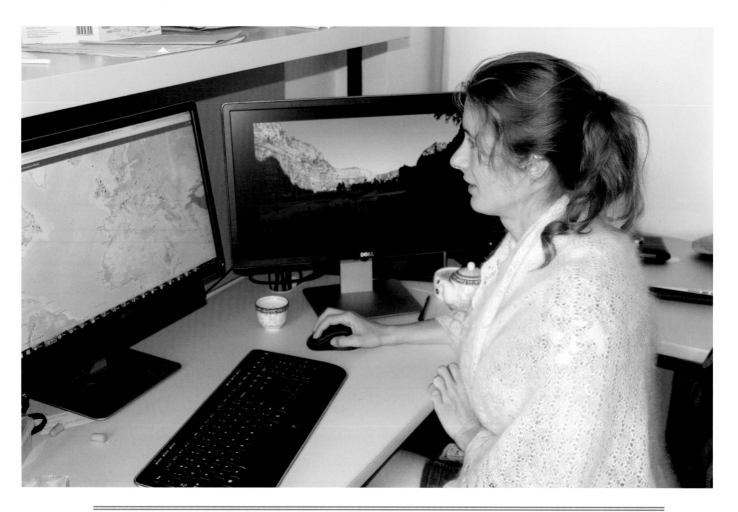

▲ *Eugenia Bragina has been helping to assemble a world map of animals that change coat colors. She also is studying museum collections from other countries to compare coat color changes from the past to the present.*

hares they saw. "Now," Marketa says, "we are beginning to walk these same kinds of areas to record if coat color timing has changed from sixty years ago in these animals." This study will test whether natural selection has *already* caused some hares to adapt to changing snow conditions—and how quickly other coat-color-changing populations might follow suit.

In a similar kind of study, Scott's colleague Dr. Eugenia Bragina is examining museum specimens to see what animal coat colors were like in the past. Originally from Russia, "Genya" studied preserved hares, weasels, lemmings, and other animals in the Zoological Museum of Moscow University, in Russia. She is also working with other international researchers to assemble a world map of animals whose coats change color. The map shows different populations of species and if they molt to white, stay brown, or are polymorphic.

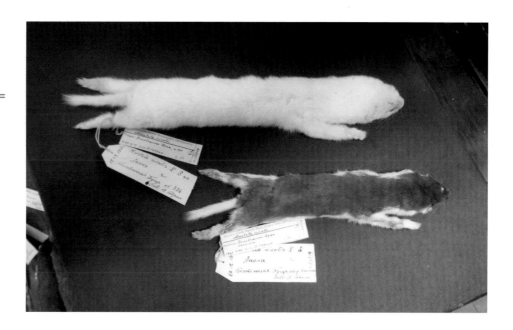

> *These pelts of least weasels, collected in the Soviet Union in 1947, may help shed light on the ability of animals to adapt to shorter winters.*

In addition to these studies, Scott and his team are working with scientists in Portugal, Ireland, Austria, and Sweden. Some of their research will investigate the molt timing of animals. Other studies will look at the actual genetics of animal populations. Every study will give scientists new insights into animals that change their coat colors, and how these animals might cope with climate change. Meanwhile, Scott is about to embark on some of his most exciting work.

^ *Rock ptarmigans are birds that inhabit polar and high-altitude regions in the northern hemisphere. Like hares, they run a greater risk of being mismatched as winters grow shorter.*

THE GENETICS OF COLOR-CHANGING COATS

*S*ome genetic traits are fairly simple and are controlled by a single gene. The ability to curl your tongue into a tube is a good example. If you inherited that gene, you can impress your friends. If you didn't get that gene, you're out of luck. Seasonal color-changing coats, however, prove to be a lot more complicated. "It's a complex trait," says Scott. "Scientists have known for a hundred years about the genetic basis of hair color. We know why your black Lab puppy is black, why your yellow Lab puppy is yellow. This is determined by genes that produce a pigment called melanin. But seasonal coat color also involves genes that respond to the length of daylight. Bringing these two traits together makes it complicated."

To better understand coat-color genetics, Scott is working with colleagues in Portugal and Montana. They are focusing on hare populations in the Cascade Mountains of Washington, where both white and brown hares can be found in winter. "It's going to take a lot more work," Scott says, "but already we are finding some interesting results. We hope that eventually we will be able to identify a collection of genes that controls seasonal coat color. Once we do that, we can go back to museum collections and see if these genes have actually changed during the past century. That will help tell us if evolution has already been taking place during the era of climate change."

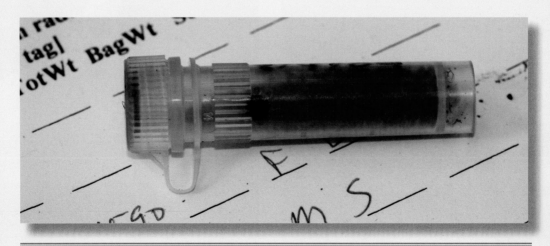

▲ *To perform genetic studies, Scott's team removes a tiny plug of flesh from the ears of captured hares.*

Welcome to the Bunny Chiller

In addition to working at the University of Montana, Scott has taught and conducted research at North Carolina State University in Raleigh. There, he built a lab consisting of four rooms in which he and his team can control day length and temperature. Scott calls the new facility the Phenotron. Others call it the "Bunny Chiller."

^ *The Phenotron, also known as the Bunny Chiller, allows Scott's team to control daylight and temperature for experiments on hare molting and behavior.*

❮ Dr. Diana Lafferty is Scott's hare whisperer. She is in charge of keeping captured hares happy and healthy, and performing behavioral experiments in the Phenotron. Here, she holds "enrichment toys" that keep hares from getting bored or stressed in their cages.

When the new lab was complete, Scott brought back hares from Montana and Washington. Now, his team is beginning to run experiments with the hares. Dr. Diana Lafferty is Scott's "hare whisperer." She is in charge of keeping the hares happy, and overseeing experiments with them. The first experiments will attempt to discover whether mismatched hares actually know if they are mismatched.

Diana explains, "We'll build two frames on the floor. On one we'll place soil and pine needles. On the other, we'll place artificial snow. Using a video camera, we'll actually be able to see how much time each hare spends on snow versus on the brown earth. We can also introduce the sounds or smells of predators. If white hares know they're mismatched, then they should go hide on the white background. If they don't know, then maybe they'll stay on the brown background because it's warmer or for some other reason we haven't figured out."

In the Phenotron, Scott also hopes to breed some of the hares so that he can discover more about their genetics and their abilities to adapt to environmental changes. Scientists will be able to combine this information with other data from around the globe to learn about the evolution of animals with seasonal coat color changes and their prospects for survival.

❯ *This humorous sign at the Phenotron reminds researchers to watch their fingers when handling hares.*

Chapter Eight

A RISKY EXPERIMENT

hile Scott runs experiments on snowshoe hares, human beings are running a much riskier experiment with our planet. Our widespread use of coal, gas, and oil for energy continues to dump huge amounts of carbon dioxide into Earth's atmosphere. According to the Environmental Protection Agency, between the years 1990 and 2013, the United States alone released between 5,000 and 6,000 *million metric tons* of carbon dioxide into the atmosphere each year (a metric ton equals 2,204 pounds). Except for China, the US produces more carbon dioxide than any other country in the world. What's more, today's levels of CO_2 in the atmosphere are higher than they have been in the last 800,000 years.

Although Scott is optimistic that snowshoe hares can survive, he realizes that climate change will have a huge impact on hares and thousands of other species. Snowshoe hare populations in Washington,

❮ *The future of hares like this one may depend on how quickly humans wean ourselves off of fossil fuels and protect hare habitat.*

CO₂ EMISSIONS OVER THE LAST 800,000 YEARS

CO₂ reading as of May 30, 2016: 407.46 parts per million

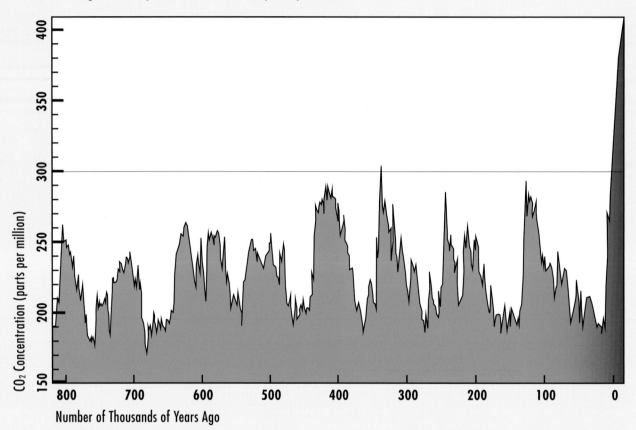

To measure past atmospheric carbon dioxide levels, scientists use several different methods, including testing air bubbles trapped in the ice from ancient glaciers in Greenland, Antarctica, and elsewhere. Starting in 1958, scientists began measuring CO₂ levels directly at an observatory on Mauna Loa volcano in Hawaii. Together, this data shows that CO₂ has fluctuated during the course of history. Recent greenhouse gas increases, however, dwarf other changes in the last 800,000 years.

Source: Scripps Institution of Oceanography, U.C. San Diego, https://scripps.ucsd.edu/programs/keelingcurve

for instance, where some hares already stay brown in winter, may be able to adapt to warmer temperatures and less snow cover. Hare populations in Montana, where all the snowshoe hares molt to white in winter, may not fare so well. They may disappear entirely.

> In many countries, wind energy has already made a significant impact in reducing our use of fossil fuels.

Without the "cheeseburger of the forest," lynx and other predators may decline or disappear, too. With fewer predators, populations of browsing animals could explode, overgrazing the forest and preventing new tree growth. The overall results are impossible to predict, but may trigger a domino effect that ripples through the entire ecosystem, affecting animals, plants—even human beings, who depend on healthy forests to protect water supplies, and provide timber, game, recreation, and many other resources.

Species around the world face similar challenges. But while it is certain that temperatures will continue to rise, Scott and other scientists also believe that there is a lot humans can do to help hares and other animal species.

Cleaner Energy

The major thing people can do to help hares and other animals is to reduce our consumption of fossil fuels. About eighty percent of energy used in the United States is generated by burning fossil fuels. Every time we ride in a car,

^ *Ski resorts such as this one provide wonderful recreational opportunties for people, but often destroy important hare habitat.*

flick on a computer, or turn on a heater, we contribute to global warming. On the flip side, riding your bike, turning off computers, or putting on a sweater instead of cranking up the thermostat—all of these actions directly reduce levels of carbon dioxide and the impacts of climate change.

But as a society we can do more. One of the most important steps is to demand that politicians work toward switching industries to renewable energy sources—those that do not release carbon dioxide or other harmful pollution. Wind and solar power are among our cleanest energy sources, and they are already making a difference. In the United States in 2004, renewable energy accounted for 8.8% of our electricity generation. By 2013, that percentage rose to 13.1%, mostly because of an increase in wind energy production. During the same time, our use of coal—our dirtiest source of electricity—dropped from 49.7% to 38.9%.

Burning gasoline for cars produces about half of US carbon dioxide emissions. Improving mileage standards for cars and trucks so that they use less gasoline may be where we can make the most progress in reducing emissions. The Obama Administration helped spearhead the drive for cleaner cars and other vehicles; new regulations should double the fuel efficiency of automobiles by the year 2025. These and other efforts may not stop climate change, but they will help lessen and slow down the process—giving snowshoe hares and other species more time to adapt.

Protecting Habitats

Meanwhile, Scott and other scientists believe that it is important to directly help animals as much as possible. One of the best ways to do this is to protect their habitats, the places where they live. Improving logging practices in places where hares are abundant, for instance, can help give the hares a better chance to survive. Restricting the construction of vacation homes, ski resorts, and other development in hare habitats would also help. So would preserving wild corridors between hare habitats so that hares can move freely from one place to another. This would give them better opportunities to spread genes that may allow them to adapt to shorter winters.

All of these steps could prevent hares and many other species from sliding toward extinction. The snowshoe hare is a quiet little animal, but it plays a big role on our planet. By studying it, Scott and his colleagues are helping answer vital questions not only about the hare's future, but about the future of many other species, including humans. With this knowledge, we can take actions that will help animals and the entire planet, making the future a brighter, healthier—and hoppier—place.

The End

Hop Up to the Plate

It's impossible for any one person to fix climate change. Each person, however, can improve the situation. In addition to reducing your own energy usage at home and in your mode of transportation, here are some less obvious ways to reduce your carbon footprint.

- **Buy less stuff and better stuff.** All stuff requires energy to make. Many times, the things we buy are soon discarded. When you're about to buy something, ask yourself, "Am I really going to use this a lot?" If the answer is no, then save some energy—and cash—and skip it. If you decide you need it, then buy an item of better quality so that it will last longer.

- **Bring your own bags.** When you shop, bring a bag from home or tell the cashier, "No, thanks. I don't need a bag." Both paper and plastic bags take energy to make. They take additional energy to recycle or bury in a landfill.

- **Close windows and doors.** When the air-conditioner or heater is running, close windows and doors to prevent these devices from having to work harder and consume more energy.

- **Install fluorescent or LED light bulbs in your house.** These bulbs use far less electricity than standard incandescent light bulbs, and they last a lot longer.

- **Urge your parents to buy cars and appliances that use less energy.** Over its lifetime, a gas-guzzling SUV or truck can use three or four times the energy of an average economy car. These larger vehicles also take much more energy to make. The same goes for refrigerators, televisions, and other appliances.

- **Eat less meat.** Meat production consumes more energy, water, and other resources than any other form of food production. Every time you eat a salad instead of a cheeseburger, you are reducing CO_2 emissions.

- **Join a group that promotes clean energy, efficient transportation, and conservation.** Here are a few groups that I like:

1. The Union of Concerned Scientists
   http://www.ucsusa.org
2. World Resources Institute
   http://www.wri.org
3. Friends of the Earth, **http://www.foe.org**
4. Natural Resources Defense Council
   http://www.nrdc.org

- **Share your knowledge with others.** Educate your friends and family about climate change and saving energy. This multiplies your own positive contribution to the planet.

Bound to the Head of the Class

Several books mention the impact of climate change on wildlife. Many others address climate change and global warming. If you want to get really smart, check out the sources listed below. Also, be sure to watch the awesome video of Brandon Davis taking Scott's dog, Sage, out to "test" snowshoe hares!

Books

- Collard, Sneed B., III. *Global Warming: A Personal Guide to Causes and Solutions.* Kalispell, MT: Lifelong Learning, Inc., 2011.

- Delano, Marfe Ferguson. *Earth in the Hot Seat: Bulletins from a Warming World.* Washington, DC: National Geographic, 2009.

- Lourie, Peter. *The Polar Bear Scientists.* Boston: Houghton Mifflin Books for Children, 2012.

- Swinburne, Stephen R. *The Sea Turtle Scientist.* Boston: Houghton Mifflin Harcourt, 2014.

- Carson, Mary Kay. *Park Scientists: Gila Monsters, Geysers, and Grizzly Bears in America's Own Backyard.* Boston: Houghton Mifflin Harcourt, 2014

Videos

• College of Forestry and Conservation at the University of Montana. "Snowshoe Hare Research." YouTube video, 7:26. March 21, 2016. https://www.youtube.com/watch?v=tOUEgqyGnrw

A short introduction of the field work with hares done by the Mills lab.

• Eye Spy Productions Pty Ltd. *Life on the Reef* (3-part series), Aired by PBS on August 5, 2015. http://video.pbs.org/program/life-reef/

Explores several consequences that climate change has had on sea turtles and the coral reef ecosystem.

Websites

Any web search will reveal thousands of websites related to climate change. Some of these—especially those sponsored by the oil and gas industry or certain other special-interest groups—are based on inaccurate or false information. They are intended to convince people that climate change is not happening, and that we should keep burning fossil fuels. However, below are three websites with the best up-to-date, scientific information on this important topic.

• EPA, United States Environmental Protection Agency. "Climate Change." March 21, 2016. http://www.epa.gov/climatechange/
Loads of information on climate change in the United States and around the world—includes kids' pages.

• National Oceanic and Atmospheric Administration, United States Department of Commerce. "Climate." March 21, 2016. http://www.noaa.gov/climate.html
Offers temperature data by year and other terrific information on climate change, including tips on reducing its impacts.

• Union of Concerned Scientists. "Science for a Healthy Planet and Safer World." March 21, 2016. http://www.ucsusa.org
One of the best sources on climate science and what we can do to combat climate change.

Hare-y Words

adapt: to adjust to new or different conditions

camouflage: colors or patterns that blend in with surroundings

carbon footprint: the greenhouse gases generated to support an individual's—or nation's—activities

carbon sink: a process or thing that removes carbon dioxide from the atmosphere; plants, for instance, naturally absorb carbon dioxide as a part of photosynthesis and store that carbon in their leaves, stems, roots, and trunks

climate change: shifting worldwide weather patterns and other changes that occur as a result of the increase in carbon dioxide and certain other heat-trapping gases emitted into the atmosphere; see also, global warming

colleagues: people with whom a person works

data: information collected by scientists

DNA: (short for deoxyribonucleic acid) molecules in our cells that hold the instructions for how we grow, function, reproduce, and most other things we do to survive

emissions: discharge, especially gases produced by burning fuels and other materials

evolve: to change, usually in response to new challenges, conditions, or opportunities

fossil fuels: sources of energy (especially oil, coal, and natural gas) created by plants and other dead organisms that have been subjected to great pressure and heat over long periods of time

genes: sections of DNA that perform specific tasks, such as determining coat colors

genetics: the composition of the genes and their properties that an organism can pass on to its offspring; also the study of DNA, genes, and their roles in individuals and populations

global warming: the heating up of Earth's atmosphere, mainly due to the burning of fossil fuels; see also, climate change

grant money: in science, money that is provided to a scientist so that she or he can conduct research studies

mismatch(ed): for an animal, having a skin or coat color that is not camouflaged with its surroundings

model: a formula that can help a scientist predict what will happen in the future, or under different sets of circumstances

molt: replacing one kind or color of fur or skin for another

natural selection: the process through which certain individuals become better adapted to their environment, allowing them to be more successful than others at surviving and passing those survival traits to their offspring

polymorphic populations: a portion of a group that contains a mix of properties, such as hair colors

population: a well-defined group or subset of individuals within a species

radio collar: a band with a built-in transmitter that sends out a signal so that scientists can locate it

renewable energy: energy that does not deplete our natural resources or do harm to the planet—especially wind, solar, geothermal, and hydroelectric energy

technician: a worker with special skills who performs certain tasks

temperate (zone or region): the milder parts of the planet between the tropics and the polar regions; the lower 48 states lie entirely within the temperate zone

threatened: endangered; the possibility of being harmed or killed or driven to extinction

trait: a quality, property, or characteristic, usually belonging to an individual

Index

Thanks!

I never could have hopped into this project without the commitment, cooperation, and humor of Professor Scott Mills, his students, colleagues, and family. Professor Mills not only let me accompany him into the field on numerous occasions, but also provided free access to his research, photos, colleagues, and students. And speaking of those, I am grateful to the following other scientists who helped this book come together: Professor Steve Running, Marketa Zimova, Alex Kumar, Brandon Davis, Dr. Eugenia Bragina, Dr. Diana Lafferty, and Professor Paulo Alves. I am especially lucky to have worked with two wonderful editors, Randi Rivers and Harold Underdown, to help make my words leap off the page, and designer Kathleen Herlihy-Paoli, who yet again turned text and images into a thing of beauty. Big thanks to Dick Moberg and Andy Howard for the generous use of their photos. Finally, and always, my love and thanks to my family, who provide the enthusiasm and support I need to keep bounding forward.

About the Hopper—um, Author

Sneed B. Collard III graduated with honors in biology from the University of California at Berkeley and earned his masters in scientific instrumentation from UC Santa Barbara. Since then, he has written more than seventy-five books for young people ranging from award-winning picture books to science books and novels. His 2015 title *Fire Birds—Valuing Natural Wildfires and Burned Forests* (Bucking Horse Books) earned a host of accolades, including being named a Junior Library Guild selection and a Eureka Honor Book by the California Reading Association. Sneed's upcoming science titles include books on insects and gliding animals. To learn more about Sneed, visit his website www.sneedbcollardiii.com and the website of Bucking Horse Books, www.buckinghorsebooks.com. Also, check out his YouTube channel for book trailers and more.